Animals of the Night

RACCOONS AFTER DARK

Ruth O'Shaughnessy

Enslow Publis
101 W. 23rd Street
Suite 240
New York, NY 10011
USA

enslow.com

Words to Know

adapt—To survive in a new place.

Algonquin—An American Indian group.

carnivore—An animal that eats meat.

den—The home of an animal.

hibernate—To sleep deeply through the winter.

nocturnal—Active at night.

omnivore—An animal that eats both meat and plants.

predator—An animal that hunts other animals for food.

rabid—Having been infected with rabies.

rabies—A disease that attacks the brain and spinal cord.

Contents

A Masked Bandit

Imagine being sound asleep in your bedroom. Suddenly, in the middle of the night, you hear a loud crash and then rustling coming from your backyard. It sounds like a stray cat has knocked over the garbage can and is now looking through the trash for food.

You are not the only one who heard it. The dog starts barking and you and your parents go check it out. You are surprised to see that it is not a cat at all! The small furry animal looks up at you with a piece of food between its paws. It is a raccoon!

How Raccoons Look

A raccoon is very easy to recognize. It is best known for the black mask around its eyes and the rings around its bushy tail. It also has short oval ears, a pointed snout, and a black nose.

Another special feature is a raccoon's front paws, which look like thin human hands. Each paw has five fingers. These fingers let raccoons do many things, such as turn a doorknob, open a refrigerator door, or even turn on a water faucet!

Fun Fact!

Raccoon comes from the Algonquin (al-gon-kwen) Indian word *aroughcoune,* which means "he scratches with his hand."

Raccoons are best known for the black mask on their faces.

Raccoons are between 2 and 3 feet (²/₃ to 1 meter) long, including the 10-inch (25-centimeter) ringed tail. Males are usually larger than females. Raccoons in the north tend to be larger than raccoons in the south as well. Raccoons come in different colors. Although they usually have long, thick grayish fur, raccoons in some parts of the United States have reddish-brown fur. A raccoon's belly is light colored.

In addition to their black face masks, raccoons also have ringed tails and handlike paws.

How Raccoons Act

Raccoons are at least as smart as dogs and cats. They communicate by hissing, whistling, screaming, and growling. They are also strong for their size and very athletic. They can quickly climb up or down a tree, swim well, and run up to 15 miles (24 kilometers) per hour.

Raccoons do not go out looking for trouble, but if cornered, they will fight fiercely. If attacked by a dog, a raccoon will rip at its body with teeth and claws. Raccoons have killed dogs.

Fun Fact!

A raccoon can easily lift a dime out of a shirt pocket with its fingers.

A raccoon uses its teeth and claws to defend itself against an attacker.

Where Raccoons Live

Raccoons live in Canada, the United States, Mexico, and parts of Central America. They are often found in the woods near water as well as in marshes, fields, and even in cities.

Raccoons make their homes, called **dens**, in hollow trees and burrows, or holes in the ground, left by other animals. Raccoons also live in brush piles, haystacks, caves, mines, or empty buildings. In towns and cities, raccoons may be found in chimneys, sewers, under decks, or in people's attics. They often tip over garbage cans to search for food.

Fun Fact!

Raccoons are not active during the winter. They stay in their dens. However, they are not truly hibernating, or sleeping deeply through the winter.

Three young raccoons emerge from their den in a tree.

Raccoons Are Omnivores

Raccoons belong to a group of animals called **carnivores**, or meat eaters. Dogs, cats, and bears are also included in this group. However, raccoons are really **omnivores** when it comes to their meals. They will eat both animals and plants. Raccoons are not picky. They eat turtle eggs, bird eggs, berries, nuts, and insects.

Raccoons also eat crayfish, frogs, clams, and mussels they find in shallow waters. Raccoons feel for their prey in the water with their front paws. They have also been known to grab food from bird feeders, farmers' fields, and garbage bags.

This raccoon has found
a crayfish to eat.

The raccoon's scientific name is *Procyon lotor* (Pro-see-on low-tore). *Lotor* means "the washer." Wherever they get their food, if there is water around, raccoons will dunk it in the water before eating it. It looks like raccoons are washing their food. But, it is more likely that they are just carefully feeling their food. They do this even if there is no water around. This is done to make sure there are no sharp bones or dangerous pieces in it.

Fun Fact!

When Christopher Columbus first saw a raccoon, he called it a "clownlike dog." But he was not the only one to think raccoons look like dogs! The first part of the raccoon's scientific name, *Procyon*, means "doglike."

A raccoon feels its food for anything sharp that may hurt it.

Creatures of the Night

Raccoons are **nocturnal** animals, which means they rest during the day and are active at night. They have excellent senses that allow them to move around well in the dark. They have very good night vision. A feature in the back of their eyes reflects light, making their eyes glow.

Raccoons also have great hearing, which helps them find prey after dark. It is also useful in avoiding **predators** because raccoons can hear an enemy come near them.

A family of raccoons uses their excellent senses to move around at night.

Family Life

Raccoons are usually loners. But from January to March, they come together to mate. Once a female raccoon is a year old, she is ready to mate. Males, however, do not mate until they are two years old.

About two months after mating, females give birth to four to six babies. Raccoon babies are called kits or cubs. Completely helpless, the kits are born without teeth, with their eyes shut, and with hardly any fur. They depend on their mother for everything.

The young raccoons can stand when they are a little more than a month old. But their mother does not take them out of the den until they are three or four months old. She will teach them to hunt and climb trees. They stay with their mother for about the first year of their lives. After that, they are on their own.

A mother raccoon takes care of her two babies.

Survival in the Wild

In the wild, raccoons can live up to ten years, but most only live for about two to three years. Although they are fierce fighters, raccoons do have many predators, such as coyotes, cougars, bobcats, and wolves. Large owls, foxes, and badgers go after raccoon babies. Their mothers try to protect them, but sometimes raccoon babies are killed.

Raccoons die in other ways as well. They are often run over by cars and trucks or killed by human hunters. Some also die from disease.

Fun Fact!

A group of raccoons is called a nursery.

The coyote is one of the raccoon's natural predators.

Relationship
with People

Throughout history, people have hunted and trapped raccoons. During the eighteenth century in North America, people ate raccoon meat and used the raccoon skins to make clothing. Many of them wore "coonskin" caps.

In the 1920s, raccoon fur coats were in fashion. Women also wore fancy raccoon hats.

Today, fewer people wear furs. Also, fewer people eat raccoons. However, some people still hunt them. Other people view raccoons as pests because raccoons eat fruit and vegetables from people's gardens. Raccoons sometimes build dens near people's homes as well.

Coonskin caps are still worn today.

Because some people find raccoons very cute, they keep them as pets. But this is not a good idea. They are still wild animals, and in many states, it is against the law to own a raccoon.

A wild raccoon that walks up to you or does not run away may actually be ill. Raccoons can carry diseases like **rabies**. A human can get rabies and die if bitten or scratched by a **rabid** raccoon. So, it is best to enjoy raccoons from a distance.

Fun Fact!

Although most people are familiar with the North American raccoon, there are six other types of raccoon.

A farmer catches a raccoon in his garden to be released in the woods.

Sharing the World with Raccoons

Unlike many other animals, raccoons are not in danger of dying out. Many raccoons are living in the world today. There are more raccoons every year because less and less people are killing them. Raccoons also **adapt** well to their surroundings. They will eat just about anything and build dens just about anywhere.

Because raccoons are night animals, few people see or hear them. At times, people may not even know that raccoons are living nearby. If people respect wildlife, raccoons and humans can easily live near one another.

Raccoons have
a bright future.
They are thriving
with humans,
while many other
animals are not.

Stay Safe Around Raccoons

Raccoons have fewer and fewer forests to live in because people continue to cut down trees and build homes. As raccoons lose their natural habitats, they start to come to people's yards more often. As this continues, we are likely to see still more raccoons around us. So it is important to be careful and follow some rules to stay safe:

- ☾ Do not feed raccoons. This can make them lose their fear of people.

- ☾ Use garbage cans that are hard to open or tip over. Or do not take the garbage out until the morning.

- ☾ Keep your pets indoors at night so there is less of a chance of your dog or cat running into a raccoon.

- ☾ If a you see a raccoon outside, do not go near it. Stay away and tell an adult.

- ☾ If a raccoon enters your home, stay calm, leave it alone, and find an adult.

- ☾ Raccoons often live in people's chimneys, attics, and under decks. If you notice any openings a raccoon might be able to come through, tell an adult so they can close them.

Learn More

Books

Hurtig, Jennifer. *Raccoons*. New York: Weigl, 2012.

Magby, Meryl. *Raccoons*. New York: Powerkids Press, 2013.

Otfinoski, Steven. *Raccoons*. New York: Cavendish Square, 2014.

Petrie, Kristin. *Raccoons*. Edina, Minn.: Checkerboard Library, 2015.

Web Sites

kids.sandiegozoo.org/animals/mammals/north-american-raccoon
Check out fun facts about raccoons!

kids.nationalgeographic.com/content/kids/en_US/animals/raccoon/
Learn more about raccoons and watch videos.

naturemappingfoundation.org/natmap/facts/raccoon_k6.html
Read about these masked scavengers.

Index

Published in 2016 by Enslow Publishing, LLC.
101 West 23rd Street, Suite 240, New York, NY 10011

Copyright © 2016 by the estate of Elaine Landau
Enslow Publishing materials copyright © 2016 by Enslow Publishing, LLC.

Library of Congress Cataloging-in-Publication Data
O'Shaughnessy, Ruth, author.
 Raccoons after dark / Ruth O'Shaughnessy.
  pages cm. — (Animals of the night)
 Summary: "Discusses raccoons, their behavior, and their environment"—Provided by publisher.
 Audience: Ages 8+
 Audience: Grades 4 to 6.
 Includes bibliographical references and index.
 ISBN 978-0-7660-6764-6 (library binding)
 ISBN 978-0-7660-6762-2 (pbk.)
 ISBN 978-0-7660-6763-9 (6-pack)
 1. Raccoon—Juvenile literature. 2. Nocturnal animals—Juvenile literature. 3. Animal behavior—Juvenile literature. I. Title.
 QL737.C26O83 2016
 599.76'32—dc23
                    2015009973

Printed in the United States of America

To Our Readers: We have done our best to make sure all Web site addresses in this book were active and appropriate when we went to press. However, the author and the publisher have no control over and assume no liability for the material available on those Web sites or on any Web sites they may link to. Any comments or suggestions can be sent by e-mail to customerservice@enslow.com.

Portions of this book originally appeared in the book *Raccoons: Scavengers of the Night*.

Photo Credits: Bill Draker/Getty Images, p. 15; Craig K. Lorenz/Science Source/Getty Images, p. 9; DEA/C.DANI/I.JESKE/DeAgostini/Getty Images, p. 23; Diane Shapiro/Photolibrary/Getty Images, p. 7; GK and Vikki Hart/Photographer's Choice/Getty Images, p. 3; James H. Karales/Photolibrary/Getty Images, p.11; kimberrywood/Digital Vision Vectors/Getty Images(green moon dingbat); narvikk/E+/Getty Images (starry background); Peter McCabe/AFP/Getty Images, p. 27; photographybyjw/moment open/Getty Images (raccoon), p. 1; Rolf Nussbaumer/Getty Images, p. 17; samxmed/E+/Getty Images (moon folios and series logo); Sidney Bahrt/Science Source/Getty Images, p. 19; Steve & Dave Maslowski/Science Source/Getty Images, p. 13; Steve Maslowski/Science Source/Getty Images, pp. 5, 21; Thomas Kitchin & Victoria Hurst/First Light/Getty Images, p. 29; Wendi Andrews/Moment/Getty Images, p. 25.

Cover Credits: photographybyjw/Open Moments/Getty Images (raccoon); narvikk/E+/Getty Images (starry backgroud) kimberrywood/Digital Vision Vectors/Getty Images (green moon dingbat); samxmeg/E+/Getty Images (moon).